Read Mark in 30 Days

Andrew Page

VTR
Publications

ISBN 978-3-95776-098-2

Cover design: Chris Allcock / VTR Publications

Introduction

It often happens.

Someone hears about Jesus being God in human form, and thinks *Is it true?*

If that's you, here are three things you might do...

1. Go to a Christianity Explored course or an Alpha course. Ask around and someone will point you in the right direction.

2. Go and see the Mark Drama: it's a dramatic presentation of the whole of Mark's Gospel.

3. Read Mark's Gospel for yourself. It's almost certainly the first of the four Gospels in the New Testament to be written. As you read it, ask yourself the question: Is it true?

In this booklet I have suggested how you might read Mark's Gospel over the next month. There's a short passage from Mark to read for each day, followed by some comments from me.

I hope you will give it a try!

Andrew Page

Day 1 – Read Mark 1:1-8

Mark's introduction to his Gospel is all about who Jesus is.

What John thinks (4-8)

Talking about Jesus, John the Baptist says that the one he is preparing the way for is incredibly important (7) and is able to put God's life inside us (8).

But there is something else too.

By linking his baptism with sins being forgiven (4-5), John is saying that Jesus is going to do something about the problem of sin and so put us right with God.

What Mark thinks (1-3)

Mark's first sentence couldn't be clearer (1). Jesus is the Messiah – the one God had promised to send, to save us from our sins.

And he's also the Son of God, who shows us what God is like.

But if you look closely at the Old Testament passages Mark quotes from (2-3), you will see that the person John the Baptist is preparing the way for is *the Lord* (3) – God himself.

What you think

Do you agree with John and Mark? Mark has written his Gospel to help us make up our own minds.

Who do *you* think Jesus is?

If you want to pray...

Tell God what you think about Jesus.

Ask God to help you make your mind up over this next month about who Jesus is and why Jesus came.

Day 2 – Read Mark 1:9-20

Mark tells us here about the first things Jesus does in his public ministry.

Baptism and temptation of Jesus (9-13)

As Jesus is baptised, God the Father tells us who Jesus is (11). If you look at those words you will see how proud he is of his Son.

But if Jesus was loved by his Father so much, why did he send him into the world?

Jesus proclaims the good news (14-15)

The kingdom of God isn't a geographical territory. It's wherever men and women turn from their sin and acknowledge that Jesus is their saviour.

Do you think you are inside God's kingdom or outside it (15)?

Jesus calls the first disciples (16-20)

Becoming a follower of Jesus means leaving something (18, 20) and deciding that he is more important than everything else.

Mark tells us this story because he wants us to consider doing what Simon, Andrew, James and John do.

If you want to pray...

Tell God you want to know if becoming a disciple of Jesus is a good thing to do.

Ask God to convince you that following Jesus is the best thing that could ever happen to anyone.

Day 3 – Read Mark 1:21-45

Today Mark tells us about four incidents in which there is no human opposition to Jesus.

Jesus drives out an evil spirit (21-28)

The people in the synagogue don't know who Jesus is, but the powers of evil do (24). And they are afraid that Jesus will destroy them. What the people do recognise is that Jesus teaches with authority (22, 27). In other words, he knows what he is talking about.

Jesus heals Simon's mother-in-law (29-34)

Whether in private (29-31) or in public (32-34) Jesus heals people or sets them free from evil *effortlessly* (31, 34). And he tells the demons to be quiet (34) because he wants people to reach their own conclusions about who he is.

Jesus says his priority is teaching (35-39)

Simon and his friends want Jesus to go back and do more miracles (37). But Jesus says there is something more important: he wants to proclaim the truth about God, sin and us. He even says this is the reason he has come into the world (38). If he is right, we need to listen to him.

Jesus heals a leper (40-45)

Jesus *feels* something when he sees this man's desperation (41), which is why he touches him. And that doesn't result in Jesus catching leprosy, but in the man catching wholeness. Jesus is more infectious than the disease.

If you want to pray…

Tell God what you think about Jesus, having read this passage today.

Ask God to help you to come to Jesus and to tell him what is on your mind (30, 36, 40). Ask him to help you listen to Jesus (38).

Day 4 – Read Mark 2:1-28

Yesterday we read four incidents with no opposition to Jesus; today in chapter 2 there are four incidents with massive opposition. And it comes from the religious leaders of all people.

Jesus heals a paralysed man (1-12)

When the paralysed man comes down through the roof, everyone thinks Jesus will just heal him. But Jesus says there is something much more important (5). It's easier to *say* 'Your sins are forgiven' because there is no visible proof that it's happened; so when Jesus heals the man he is proving that he can forgive sins (10-12). If that's true, it means that Jesus is God (6-7). What do *you* think?

Jesus calls Levi and eats with sinners (13-17)

The religious leaders think that good people shouldn't mix with sinners like Levi and his friends (16). But Jesus replies that that would be like a doctor refusing to have any contact with sick people (17a). Just as a doctor comes to help the sick, Jesus came to rescue sinners (17b).

Jesus predicts a break with Judaism (18-22)

The religious leaders think good people should be religious (18), but Jesus says he is like the bridegroom at a wedding: when he is around, people should be feasting, not fasting (19). The religious leaders are like old wineskins, which will not be able to contain Jesus, who is the new wine (22a). Instead, Jesus is looking for new wineskins – people who will welcome him and celebrate with him. How do you feel about welcoming Jesus?

Jesus is Lord of the Sabbath (23-28)

According to the religious leaders, taking off a few ears of corn is harvesting (23-24). But Jesus tells them they have the wrong idea about what the Sabbath is for (27). And then he makes a massive claim about himself: *he* has the right to decide how people should behave on the Sabbath, or on any other day for that matter (28). Who does this man Jesus think he is?

If you want to pray...

Tell God whether you are on the side of the religious leaders or on the side of Jesus – or if you are not sure.

Ask God to show you that your greatest need is to have your sins forgiven (5) – and that Jesus can do that for you.

Day 5 – Read Mark 3:1-12

Today the opposition to Jesus becomes even more extreme. But he becomes more popular too.

Jesus provokes opposition (1-6)

Jesus is deliberately doing this miracle openly on the Sabbath (3), because he knows he is being watched (2). His question (4) is designed to persuade his enemies to think again, but they are having none of it (4-5). So after the healing the decision is reached to get rid of Jesus (6).

Jesus' growing popularity (7-12)

Although the religious leaders are opposed to Jesus, many ordinary people are on his side (7-8). But it looks like they are mainly looking for miracles (10). This is why Jesus decides to teach from a boat, so that the people will listen to what he has to say (9-10 – see also chapter 4:1).

Looking back on what you have read so far in Mark's Gospel, what do you want from Jesus – miracles or the truth?

If you want to pray...

Tell God if you are willing to listen to what Jesus has to say to you.

Ask God to help you to respond positively to Jesus and to listen to his teaching as you keep reading through Mark.

Day 6 – Read Mark 3:13-35

At the same time as Jesus is choosing 12 of his followers to be his apostles, the opposition is growing. It comes from those who know him best and from those who know Jewish religion best.

Jesus chooses the 12 apostles (13-19)

Jesus is going to train this team and then send them out to be his representatives (*apostles* means *sent ones*). But the first reason Jesus calls them is so that they will spend time with him (14). That is his priority for us too.

Opposition from the family (20-21)

Jesus' determination to spread his message means meals are being missed. So his family are worried about him. Their love for Jesus makes them want to distract him from what matters most.

Opposition from the religious leaders (22-30)

When the religious leaders decide that Jesus is possessed by an evil spirit, Jesus shows them that their position is illogical (23-26). And now he explains what is really happening (27) by using a short parable. We are prisoners of Satan (the devil) until Jesus attacks him and sets us free.

And Jesus finishes with a warning (28-30): some sins can make a person so hard that they no longer want forgiveness, and so remain unforgiven for ever.

Opposition from the family (31-35)

When the family arrive to take charge of Jesus, he explains that he has a new family – people who want to live God's way (34-35).

If you want to pray...

Tell God how you feel about this idea of you being a prisoner of the devil.

Ask God to show you that Jesus can set you free to be the person he designed you to be.

Day 7 – Read Mark 4:1-34

Most of us would like to change. Today, Jesus tells four parables. They explain that what changes human lives more than anything else is the word of God.

The sower (1-20)

There are four kinds of human heart, and that affects how we react when God speaks to us: hard hearts (4, 15); shallow hearts (5-6, 16-17); over-crowded hearts (7, 18-19); and open hearts (8, 20). What is your heart like? Would you like God to change your heart?

The lamp (21-25)

When Jesus teaches it's like a lamp shining into our lives, showing us what we're really like (21-22). And Jesus encourages us too: if we respond positively to what we have understood so far, we'll understand more and more (25).

The seed growing secretly (26-29)

When we're reading Mark's Gospel we may think that there is nothing happening inside us. But, says Jesus, there is so much power in God's word that we can be sure that he is at work – even if we are not aware of it yet (28).

The mustard seed (30-34)

Reading Mark's Gospel may seem pretty unspectacular. But look what happens to the unspectacular mustard seed (32). Once again, Jesus' message is clear: there is immense power in the word of God.

If you want to pray...

Tell God if you believe he can use the Bible to change your heart and your life. And tell him what your heart is like today – hard, shallow, over-crowded or open.

Ask God to keep using Mark's Gospel in your life so that you will understand the good news about Jesus more and more clearly.

Day 8 – Read Mark 4:35 - 5:43

Yesterday we heard four parables; today we will see four miracles. The extraordinary power of Jesus should make us ask ourselves a crucial question (4:41).

Jesus calms a storm (4:35-41)

Look at the power of Jesus' words: when he speaks to the wind and the waves, they obey him (39). If you look carefully at what Jesus says (40), you will see that the disciples are more frightened *after* the storm than they were *during* it. The reason is that they are wondering who it is who can do things like this (41).

Jesus drives out Legion (5:1-20)

Whatever we may think about evil spirits, this man is out of control (3-4). Mark makes it clear that the demons can do only what Jesus allows them to (12-13). The local people are terrified when they see how Jesus is capable of changing someone (15), and ask him to leave (17). People still do that today.

Jesus heals a sick woman (5:25-34)

This healing, sandwiched inside the story of a dead girl being raised to life, shows that Jesus is so powerful that this sick woman is healed just by touching him (27-29). Jesus waits until she tells him the whole truth (34); he wants us to do the same thing.

Jesus raises a dead girl to life (5:21-43)

In the first three miracles Mark has shown us that Jesus has power over nature, evil and sickness; here we see that he even has power over death. Notice that some people reject Jesus' words (38-40), but that these words have great power (40-42).

If you want to pray...

Tell God if you want to find the answer to the disciples' question 'Who is this man?' (4:41).

Ask God to help you receive Jesus' words instead of rejecting them (5:40); and to welcome him into your life instead of sending him away (5:17).

Day 9 – Read Mark 6:1-6

Today's short passage is like a summary of the story so far. It is a good opportunity to take stock of where we have got to.

Opposition from family and friends (1-6)

Jesus is in his home town of Nazareth, teaching in the synagogue. But, once again, those who know him best are rejecting him (2-3). For Jesus the major problem seems to be that they refuse to trust him: he is looking for people to have faith in him (6; see also 2:5, 4:40 and 5:34, 36).

Thinking back to everything you have read so far in this Gospel, what has struck you most? Which incidents do you like most? Are there any which disturb you?

Now that you have read Mark's Gospel up to this point, do you find it easier or harder to trust Jesus?

If you want to pray...

Tell God how you feel about Jesus, and especially about who he is.

Ask God to keep using Mark's Gospel in your life, to show you who Jesus is and why he came – and how you can experience him for yourself.

Day 10 – Read Mark 6:7-33

This is another example of Mark sandwiching one story inside another. Here, the story of Jesus sending out the apostles (7-13) and their return (30-33) is on either side of the account of the death of John the Baptist.

Jesus sends out the Twelve (7-13)

Jesus is determined to place the apostles in a situation in which they are out of their depth (8). This will force them to trust him. And although he is not with them physically, they experience Jesus using them (13) and bringing people back to God through their message (12).

The death of John the Baptist (14-29)

This paragraph begins with a reminder that people are still trying to work out who Jesus is (14-16). The story of Herod's birthday party and his stupid promise to his wife's daughter (21-23) leads to her asking Herod to have John the Baptist killed (24-25).

Herod doesn't want to do this, because he respects John (20). But he still gives the order for John to be beheaded. Why? He is afraid of what people will think of him if he doesn't (26).

The Twelve return to Jesus (30-33)

The apostles tell Jesus everything that has happened on their trip (30). This is another example of Jesus wanting his disciples to spend time with him (31-32; and see 3:14).

If you want to pray...

Tell God if you sometimes disobey him because you are afraid of what others will say if you try to live for him.

Ask God to help you understand who Jesus is and what it means to follow him.

Day 11 – Read Mark 6:34-56

Today Jesus encounters three groups of Jewish people – a crowd of 5,000, the 12 disciples and numerous sick people. Through it all, Jesus is training his followers to recognise who he is.

Jesus feeds the 5,000 (34-44)

Notice that Jesus thinks our greatest need is not miracles but teaching (34). But his compassion for 5,000 hungry people prompts him to feed them miraculously (38, 42).

Jesus once again brings his disciples into a situation in which they are out of their depth (37-38). When they see the miracle they should immediately realise that he is the Messiah. But their hearts are hard (52; see also 4:15).

If our hearts are hard we will fail to see what Jesus is doing in our own lives and in others' lives too.

Jesus walks on water (45-52)

This is a miracle only for the disciples: Jesus wants them to recognise who he is. He demonstrates his identity by defying gravity and walking on water (48); and he reveals his identity by saying 'I am' (50), which is the name of God in the Old Testament (see Exodus 3:14). Jesus is God in human form.

The disciples are amazed (51), but they have still not realised who Jesus is. It is possible to be amazed by Jesus but still not to understand who he is and why he came.

Jesus heals in Gennesaret (53-56)

The people here recognise Jesus as the man who can heal, and so they bring many sick people to him. They are healed as they touch him (56; see also 3:10 and 5:27-28).

We cannot touch Jesus physically, but Mark is encouraging us to deliberately trust the Son of God.

If you want to pray...

Tell God about any situation in your life which makes you feel out of your depth.

Ask God to give you an open heart so you can see what Jesus is doing in your life.

Day 12 – Read Mark 7:1-23

We have already seen that the religious leaders are opposing Jesus. Today it becomes clearer than ever that you can't describe Jesus as religious.

God's word and human tradition (1-13)

The religious leaders have rules for everything, which are called the tradition of the elders (3b).

Jesus' reaction is blunt. He calls the leaders hypocrites (6) and makes it very clear that their traditions are man-made and not from God (7, 8, 9, 13). In fact keeping human rules is more important to them than obeying God (8, 9).

For example, says Jesus: Your rule about calling your money 'corban' (devoted to God) results in your disobeying God's command to honour your parents (10-12).

So here's the principle: God's word in the Bible has authority but human rules don't. And being religious can result in saying the right things but being miles away from God in your heart (6b).

What makes people unclean? (14-23)

The religious leaders think you make yourself dirty in God's sight by eating the wrong food; Jesus says they're wrong (14-19). Earlier in the Gospel they criticised Jesus for going to Levi's party (see 2:13-17).

According to Jesus, what makes us 'unclean' is the stuff that comes out of our hearts (20-23). None of us can honestly read that list of sins (21-22) without admitting that we have been guilty of some of these things.

Jesus is reminding us that all of us are guilty and need forgiveness; but Mark has already made it clear that Jesus can give us the forgiveness we need (see 2:10).

One last thought: Did you notice that Jesus *doesn't* say that evil things come out of *our* hearts (21)? He knows that *his* heart doesn't contain any of these sins.

If you want to pray...

Tell God whether you agree that that list of sins describes your heart (21-22).

Ask God to help you not to follow religious rules, but to follow Jesus by obeying God's word.

Day 13 – Read Mark 7:24 – 8:10

After three encounters with Jewish people (6:34-56) and a confrontation with the religious leaders (7:1-23), Jesus now has three encounters with Gentiles, i.e. people who are not Jewish. This should shock us: in the first century Gentiles were the outsiders; most Jews avoided all contact with them.

Jesus and the Syro-Phoenician woman (24-30)

Jesus' response to the woman's request (26) hardly sounds friendly (27). But his use of the word 'first' (27) implies that there will be a time when Gentiles will be invited to know God. Her brilliant answer (28) seems to persuade Jesus to grant her request (29). Notice, too, that it is no problem for Jesus to do this miracle from a distance (30).

Jesus heals a deaf and dumb man (7:31-37)

Jesus takes this man aside (33) because he treats people as individuals and is willing to take time for us. And he does a number of things to help this man expect a miracle (33-34).

Jesus feeds the 4,000 (8:1-10)

The disciples have already seen Jesus feed a huge crowd (see 6:34-44). But they seem to have forgotten it already (4). What we need to remember is that this crowd are Gentiles.

If you ever feel like an outsider, what we have read today should fill us with hope. This extraordinary man Jesus seems to avoid the religious and have time for the outsiders.

And, above everything else, he wants us to see who he is.

If you want to pray...

Tell God how you feel about Jesus, now that Mark's portrait of him becomes clearer and clearer.

Ask God to help you decide who Jesus is. There is nothing more important.

Day 14 – Read Mark 8:11-30

Today we come to the halfway stage in Mark's Gospel, as the disciples recognise who Jesus is.

The Pharisees demand a sign (11-13)

The religious leaders' request (11) is not an honest one: they have no intention of following Jesus. And so Jesus refuses to respond (12).

If we are honest doubters, Jesus will answer our questions. But he has no time for professional sceptics.

The confusion of the disciples (14-21)

There may be a Mark joke in this paragraph. The disciples have no bread (16), but Mark says they have one loaf with them in the boat (14). Could this be Jesus, who satisfies our deepest needs?

The disciples remember the details of the two feedings (17-21), but they don't yet see who Jesus is. They are still spiritually blind (18).

The two-stage healing of a blind man (22-26)

This man is physically blind; and his healing is a process (23-25).

The same is true for everyone who wants to discover the truth about Jesus. It's a process: it's as if Jesus is putting his hands on our spiritual eyes (23, 25).

Peter's confession of Jesus (27-30)

First Jesus asks his disciples what *other* people are saying about him (27-28). But he really wants to know what *they* think (29a). Peter, on behalf of all the disciples, says Jesus is the Messiah, the saviour God had promised to send (29b).

This is a day Jesus has been looking forward to. It's a massive step forward for the disciples.

So what about *you*? Who do *you* think Jesus is?

If you want to pray...

Tell God if you would like him to help you to move from honest scepticism to real faith in Jesus.

Ask Jesus to keep putting his hands on your eyes, so you will see him more clearly.

Day 15 – Read Mark 8:31 – 9:29

Over these next few days we will see Jesus teaching his disciples. Now that they have recognised who he is (see 8:29), they need to learn why he has come.

The first prediction (8:31-33)

Jesus says he *must* suffer and die (31). When Peter resists this idea Jesus' reaction shows how determined he is not to be deflected from fulfilling his Father's plan (33).

The call to discipleship (8:34 – 9:1)

If we decide to follow a suffering Messiah we will suffer ourselves. Denying myself (34) means refusing to put myself first, and taking up my cross (34) means being ready, if necessary, to die for Jesus.

Jesus says we should not be embarrassed or ashamed about belonging to him (38). This is strong stuff.

The transfiguration (9:2-13)

Peter, James and John get to see Jesus as he really is – glorious and supernatural (2-3). God the Father speaks from heaven (7; remember 1:11?), telling us who Jesus is and how we should respond to him.

Jesus drives out an evil spirit (9:14-29)

The possessed boy's father says something to Jesus that lots of us would do well to say (24). Once again we see here that Jesus has limitless authority (25-27).

If you want to pray...

Tell God what you think about Jesus saying he *must* suffer and die.

Ask Jesus to help you overcome your unbelief (24).

Day 16 – Read Mark 9:30-50

Today it becomes even clearer that the disciples have a long way to go before they understand what it means to follow Jesus.

After the second prediction of Jesus' death, there are three mistakes disciples can easily make.

The second prediction (30-32)

Did you notice why Jesus wants to be on his own with the disciples (30-31)? But they still don't seem to understand why Jesus is talking about his death (32).

"I am the greatest" (33-37)

Just after hearing about Jesus' suffering again, the disciples are arguing about who the best disciple is (34). Jesus explains what true greatness looks like: it is serving others (35-37).

"We are the only ones" (38-41)

Now the disciples are claiming that they are the only people Jesus would ever want in his team (38). Jesus warns them not to exclude those who genuinely want to live for him (39-41).

"Sin doesn't matter" (42-50)

If we take sin lightly, says Jesus, we are playing with fire. By being thoughtless we can cause others (42) or ourselves (43-48) to trip up. The hand (43) may refer to something I do, the foot (45) to somewhere I go, and the eye (47) to something I look at.

Did you notice that Jesus says that hell is a reality (43, 45, 47-48)?

Of these three mistakes (33-50), which do you see most often in others? And in yourself?

If you want to pray...

Tell God which of these three mistakes you struggle with most.

Ask Jesus to help you actively serve other people.

Day 17 – Read Mark 10:1-31

Today Jesus identifies three areas in which those who follow him need to be radically different. The passage ends with a promise for faithful disciples.

Attitude to marriage (1-12)

Jesus turns a trick question (2) into an opportunity to talk about the importance of marriage. He quotes from the Old Testament book of Genesis (6-7), making it clear that marriage is God's idea (9). Christian disciples should take marriage seriously.

Attitude to children (13-16)

In the first century children were considered unimportant. But Jesus sees things differently (13-14). If we want to be accepted by God, we can't earn it or demand it; we must receive it as a gift (15-16).

Attitude to possessions (17-27)

The desire for material things can easily become more important to us than Jesus (21). He is not telling all would-be disciples to sell everything they have, but to make sure that he is really going to have first place in our lives (23-27).

The rewards of discipleship (28-31)

Jesus is not talking about literally leaving all of these things (29), but about our deciding not to let any of these things be more important than Jesus. These are strong words.

Following Jesus will bring opposition (30), but also a huge reward – a huge new family (other Christians) in this life and eternal life in the next (30-31).

If you want to pray...

Tell God in which of the three areas your attitude needs to change most.

Ask Jesus to help you to be willing to put him first.

Day 18 – Read Mark 10:32-52

Jesus and his disciples are approaching the climax of the story (32), but there is so much about him they have not understood.

The third prediction (32-34)

This is the most detailed prediction of the three. Jesus even mentions that people who are not Jews (Gentiles, 33) will be involved in his death too.

James and John's request (35-45)

Jesus' prediction of his suffering has fallen on deaf ears again (37). He explains to James and John that he *must* suffer – and that they will too (38-40). Now Jesus explains to all the disciples that true greatness is being a servant (41-44).

Jesus explains here for the first time the reason for his coming into the world (45) and the purpose of his death (45). He has come to set us free, to pay the price which will give us friendship with God. And this price is his own death (45).

This is perhaps the most important sentence in Mark's Gospel.

The healing of blind Bartimaeus (46-52)

Although he is blind, Bartimaeus can see something: Jesus is the Messiah (47-48). Did you notice that Jesus is willing to stop (49) when people call him to him for help? This is still true.

And see what Bartimaeus decides to do after Jesus heals him (52).

If you want to pray...

Tell God how you feel about the idea of following Jesus.

Ask Jesus to help you understand what it would mean for you to become his disciple.

Day 19 – Read Mark 11:1-25

Today is a key moment in the Gospel. Jesus comes to Jerusalem for the last time, knowing he will be crucified. Why has he made this decision to go to his death?

Jesus enters Jerusalem (1-11)

Riding into the city on a colt is the act of a humble king (7). The crowds give Jesus an enthusiastic welcome (8-10), though this is probably superficial. What do you think Jesus might be looking for in the Jewish temple (11)?

Jesus curses a fig-tree (12-14)

If there are leaves on a fig-tree there should be early, edible figs too – a sign of more fruit to come. But this tree is all leaves and no fruit (13). The intriguing thing here is that in the Old Testament the fig-tree is a symbol for the nation of Israel...

Jesus clears the temple (15-19)

Now the earlier symbolic judgment becomes real. Jesus is saying that the religion in the temple is all leaves and no fruit (17): where are the qualities you should expect to see in people who know God? And why do you think the religious leaders react so negatively to what Jesus has done (18)?

Jesus teaches about prayer from the fig-tree (20-25)

The next day Jesus talks about the fruit which was missing in the temple (17). He makes it clear that if prayer is to be real, disciples must trust God (22-24) and have healthy relationships (25). What can you do to make prayer meaningful in your life?

If you want to pray...

Tell God what you think of Jesus intervening like that in the temple.

Ask Jesus to make prayer something real in your life, not just a religious thing to do.

Day 20 – Mark 11:27 – 12:27

Today we are in the temple again. In these four incidents, watch Jesus responding to the trick questions of his enemies.

The authority of Jesus questioned (11:27-33)

The religious leaders are trying to trap Jesus (27-28). The question he asks them (29-30) puts them in a difficult position.

But the story he goes on to tell could not be clearer.

The parable of the tenants (12:1-12)

The vineyard is a picture for Israel; its owner is God; the tenant farmers are the religious leaders; and the servants the owner sends to collect the fruit are the Old Testament prophets (1-5).

The son, of course, is Jesus himself (6). What do you think Jesus is saying is going to happen very soon (7-8)? And what will God do as a result (9)?

Paying taxes to Caesar (12:13-17)

This is another trick question (13-15). The answer Jesus gives (17) is that it is right to pay taxes to the State. But what do you think Jesus is saying we should be giving to God (17)?

Marriage at the resurrection (12:18-27)

The Sadducees tell their funny story (19-23) because they want to prove how ludicrous it is to believe in life after death. But what does Jesus accuse them of (24)?

If you want to pray...

Tell God what your reaction is to the parable of the tenants.

Ask Jesus to help you respond to him in a way that is different from the way his enemies responded in this passage today.

Day 21 – Read Mark 12:28-44

Once again there are four incidents in the temple here. But today – in contrast to yesterday – the response from the people around Jesus is much more positive. The Gospel is inviting us to consider how we are reacting to him.

The greatest commandment (28-34)

Jesus clearly thinks that love to God and love to others are central to being a fulfilled human being (29-31). And the teacher of the law gets it (32-33): these two commands are more important than religious activities (33b).

A question about the Messiah (35-37)

Now Jesus is asking the questions. How can the Messiah (God's promised saviour) be both King David's son (35) and King David's lord (36-37)? Can you work out the answer?

Watch out for the teachers of the law (38-40)

What are Jesus' main criticisms of these religious leaders? It is very clear that he expects that God will judge them (40b).

The widow's offering (41-44)

Do you think Jesus is right or wrong in verse 43? He seems to be saying that what God looks at is not the amount we give but the attitude in our hearts.

If you want to pray...

Tell God which part of the teaching of Jesus you have looked at today, has impressed you most.

Ask Jesus to help you to respond to him in the right way.

Day 22 – Read Mark 13:1-37

Some of the disciples ask Jesus when the temple is going to be destroyed (4). Jesus doesn't give them a date (it actually happened in AD70).

Instead, he tells them two important things.

Two important things

First, in the lead-up to the destruction of the temple, there will be imposters (6), wars (7-8) and opposition to the followers of Jesus (9-13).

Second, at the end of history, Jesus will return to this world. No one knows when that will be (32-33).

Jesus tells us we should respond to this in two ways.

Two important reactions

First, we should take very seriously everything Jesus says (31). Are you taking his words more seriously than you did when you first started reading Mark's Gospel?

And, second, we should be alert (37), so that we are still following Jesus when he returns. What do you think Jesus means by 'watching'?

If you want to pray...

Tell God the most important things you have understood from this chapter of Mark's Gospel.

Ask Jesus to show you how you can follow him.

Day 23 – Read Mark 14:1-11

This is the beginning of the climax of the Gospel. Mark encourages us to think about our reaction to Jesus by writing these verses as a kind of sandwich...

Plans against Jesus (1-2)

The Passover was a celebration of the time when God rescued the people of Israel out of slavery in Egypt. But instead of thanking God the religious leaders are working out how they can get rid of Jesus.

The anointing in Bethany (3-9)

Here is a woman who shows Jesus how much she loves him. This may make us feel a bit uncomfortable, the way it did the disciples and the other guests; but Jesus responds completely positively (6-9).

He says that her pouring out of the perfume is *beautiful* (6) and *timely* (7). And it's *prophetic* too (8): somehow she seems to know that he is soon going to die.

And then Jesus says that what she has done is *memorable* (9). It is almost like he is saying that he will make sure that this story will be included in the Bible. Do you understand why? Jesus is telling us that it is right for us to show him love.

Plans against Jesus (10-11)

Judas' offer to betray Jesus is all the more shocking because he is 'one of the Twelve' (10).

Do you see how today's passage is a hate-love-hate sandwich? Mark is asking us the question 'How are you going to respond to Jesus?'

Now *that's* a question worth thinking about.

If you want to pray...

Tell God what you think of the different people around Jesus in this passage.

Ask Jesus to help you love him because of his great love to you.

Day 24 – Read Mark 14:12-31

This is almost the last time Jesus is alone with his disciples before being arrested and going to the cross. So what he says to them now is incredibly important.

The last supper (12-26)

This is the traditional Jewish Passover meal, at which people remembered how a lamb's death had set the nation of Israel free from slavery (12). But Jesus gives it a new twist.

Jesus tells his disciples that the bread they are eating should make them think of his body (22) and that the wine they are drinking should remind them of his blood (23).

Do you see what he is saying? He is the fulfilment of the Passover lamb; he will die so that men and women can be set free from the guilt and power of sin.

Jesus wants his disciples to begin to understand this before he goes to the cross.

He wants us to understand it too.

Jesus predicts that Peter will deny him (27-31)

Did you notice that Peter is claiming that he is better than the other disciples (29)? He is still saying that he is the greatest (see 9:33-37), but Jesus warns that Peter will deny three times that he knows him (30-31).

But Jesus is teaching his disciples two other very important things here.

First, by quoting from an ancient prophecy about the action of God, he makes clear that his death is not just a human tragedy but also a divine decision (27).

And second, Jesus reminds the disciples that he is going to rise from the dead (28). The resurrection of Jesus is going to be the proof that he has paid the price for our sins.

If you want to pray...

Tell God how you feel about the death of Jesus.

Ask Jesus to help you understand the things he is explaining to his disciples in this passage.

Day 25 – Read Mark 14:32-52

Nothing can convey Jesus' anguish adequately as he contemplates dying for the sins of the whole world.

Jesus in Gethsemane (32-42)

Jesus must feel so lonely in this garden: in his hour of greatest need, when he needs his friends most, they fall asleep (37, 40).

He warns his disciples that they must stay spiritually awake (38). But he also does nothing to hide from them the awfulness of what he is going through (34).

Three times Jesus asks God his Father to take away the cup of suffering (35-36, 39, 41). And three times the answer is No: there is no other way for sinners to be set free from the guilt and power of sin.

So Jesus makes his decision: out of love for his Father and out of love for us, he will go to the cross.

Jesus is arrested (43-52)

Once again Mark reminds us that Judas is 'one of the Twelve' (43).

Of all the signals Judas might have arranged with the religious leaders, he has chosen a kiss (44-45). But Jesus makes no attempt to escape (48-49).

Do you know why?

He has already made the decision to go to the cross, and he is convinced that 'the Scriptures must be fulfilled' (49). It is God's plan that he should die for the sins of the world, and Jesus is voluntarily submitting to that plan.

Can you imagine how Jesus feels in verse 50?

If you want to pray...

Tell God what you think of Jesus going through the anguish in the garden of Gethsemane.

Ask Jesus to help you understand why he decided to go to the cross.

Day 26 – Mark 14:53 – 15:15

Today we see Jesus on trial.

Jesus before the Jewish Council (14:53-65)

Mark makes it very clear that Jesus is innocent of all charges (55-59). So the high priest asks him a direct question (61).

Jesus' answer is enough to take your breath away (62). He is the glorious Son of Man who will be at the right hand of God: this is a claim to be fulfilling an ancient prophecy in the Bible's Book of Daniel (see Daniel 7:13-14).

But there is more. When Jesus says 'I am' (62), he is using the name of God from the Old Testament (remember chapter 6:50?). No wonder the high priest accuses him of blasphemy (63-64).

Peter denies Jesus (14:66-72)

Now Peter shows that he has not taken seriously Jesus' warning to watch and pray (see 14:38). Three times he denies all knowledge of Jesus.

The third time Peter calls down curses on himself (71). This probably means that he says 'God curse me if I'm lying!' And then he does lie, by saying again that he does not know Jesus.

Do you see what this means? Peter deserves to be cursed by God because of his sin. But Mark wants us to understand that Jesus is soon going to take the punishment instead – by dying on the cross. This is good news for all of us.

Jesus before the Roman governor (15:1-15)

Once again, Jesus makes no attempt to defend himself (3-5). But he is very open as to his identity (2).

Pilate, the Roman governor, knows that Jesus is innocent (9-10) and wants to let him go. But the crowds, whipped up by the religious leaders, demand the release of Barabbas, a murderer, instead (7, 11).

Jesus, an innocent man, is going to die in the place of a guilty one. This is the good news of the Gospel.

If you want to pray...

Tell God what you think about Jesus as we see him in today's passage.

Ask Jesus to help you understand his love for you.

Day 27 – Read Mark 15:16-39

It is no accident that the symbol of the Christian faith is a cross: on the cross Jesus is dying for our sins.

Mockery (16-20)

If Jesus really calmed a storm with a word and fed 5,000 people with five loaves and a few fish, he could defend himself now. Why does he choose not to?

Without knowing it, the soldiers are making fun of their Creator.

Crucifixion (21-32)

The drink offered to Jesus (23) is an anaesthetic, but Jesus refuses it. He is determined to go through this suffering.

What makes it worse is the taunts of the people near the cross. The rebels crucified next to Jesus and the passers-by heap insults on him (27-30, 32b), while the religious leaders mock him among themselves (31-32a).

They find it funny that although Jesus saved others he cannot save himself (31). This is so close to the truth: the reason Jesus is not saving himself is *so that* he can save others.

Death (33-39)

Jesus' question (34) can only have one answer. There is only one thing in the universe that separates a man or a woman from God, and that is sin. But Jesus had no sin of his own.

So here is the answer: It *was* sin separating Jesus from God. But it wasn't *his* sin; it was *ours*.

The curtain in the temple (38) shut sinners out from the presence of God. But when Jesus dies God tears the curtain, as if to say to any of us who will listen *You can come in now!*

A Roman centurion was used to crucifixions, but did you see his reaction to this one (39)? What do you think is different about Jesus' death?

If you want to pray...

Tell God what you find most impressive about the way Jesus faces his suffering in this passage.

Ask Jesus to help you believe that he died on the cross to save *you* from your sins.

Day 28 – Read Mark 15:40-47

Jesus is dead. Today we see the reactions of a number of people to that reality.

The women at the cross (40-41)

The male disciples have run away, but the women stand and watch. It is almost as if Mark is inviting us to do the same: to watch Jesus dying and to wonder what it all means.

A rich man who is following Jesus (42-47)

Joseph of Arimathea is 'waiting for the kingdom of God' (43), which probably means that he is a secret disciple of Jesus. And he is rich: he owns his own tomb (46).

But now he is coming out as a Jesus follower: he asks Pilate for permission to bury Jesus' body (43). This will change for ever the way other people in society will see him.

Back in chapter 14:3-9 we saw the love of one woman for Jesus. Here, at the end of chapter 15, we see the love of one man for Jesus. In chapter 14:12 – 15:39 we see the love of Jesus for us.

Mark is inviting us to think about what our response is going to be to the love of Jesus.

If you want to pray...

Tell God how you want to respond to the love of Jesus.

Ask Jesus to help you imitate the woman who anointed him and Joseph who gave up his tomb for him.

Day 29 – Read Mark 16:1-8

The death of Jesus is not the end of the story. Just as he had told his disciples, he rises from death.

What the women think (1-3)

Some women want to anoint the body of Jesus as a demonstration of their love for him. But they are nervous as to how they are going to be able to move the stone (3).

What the angel says (4-8)

First, Jesus has conquered death (6). As we have already seen, this is the proof that he has fully paid the price for our sins.

Second, they can meet the risen Jesus (7). The women are to tell the disciples so that they can see for themselves that he is no longer dead. Look at the end of the other three Gospels and you will see some examples of people meeting Jesus after his resurrection.

Third, Peter can be forgiven. Did you notice that the angel tells the women to give the resurrection message to the disciples *and Peter* (7)? If the angel had not said those two words Peter would have assumed that Jesus wanted nothing more to do with him. After all, he had denied all knowledge of his friend and master.

And so the risen Jesus said to the angel 'Make sure you say *and Peter*'.

Here it is again: this is the love of Jesus for sinners. The words *and Peter* are good news for everyone willing to admit that they are a sinner. Jesus has paid for our failures in his death and proved that in his resurrection.

If you want to pray...

Tell God if you are convinced by this account of the resurrection of Jesus.

Ask Jesus to come into your life, to bring you forgiveness and acceptance with God.

Day 30 – Mark 1:1 – 16:8

Thank you for taking time to read through Mark's Gospel.

Do you feel differently about Jesus now, compared to how you felt about him before you started using *Read Mark in 30 days*?

So what is your next step going to be?

Maybe you have big questions about whether the Christian message is true. Why not ask a friend to suggest a chapter in a book written for honest sceptics?

Maybe you have doubts about the cost of becoming a Christian. Why not talk to a Christian friend and ask them your questions?

But maybe you are ready to put your trust in Jesus. Why not read through this prayer and ask yourself if you are ready to take this important step? If the answer is Yes, then make the prayer your own, adding your own words as and when you want to.

Lord Jesus, thank you for speaking to me through Mark's Gospel…

I admit to you that I am a sinner and that I need to be forgiven by you. Here are some of the things I am ashamed of…

Lord Jesus, I believe that you are the Son of God and that you died on the cross for my sins. Thank you for loving me…

I have considered whether I am willing to follow you. I now turn from everything I know to be wrong. Please send your Holy Spirit into my life to help me live for you from now on…

And now I decide to follow you, Lord Jesus. Please come into my life as my saviour and forgive me; please come into my life as my Lord and take control; please come into my life as my friend and let me experience your presence.

Amen.

The Matthew Experiment

How Matthew's Gospel can help you know Jesus better

Andrew Page

Are you looking for a new way of getting to know Jesus better? A great place to start is to get into one of the four Gospels. This book is designed to help us to do just that. After writing books about Mark's Gospel and about John's Gospel, Andrew Page has now turned his attention to the Gospel of Matthew.

The Matthew Experiment is two things. First, it's a basic commentary: Andrew unpacks the message of Matthew by teaching through the Gospel from beginning to end. And second, it's an invitation: the book explains how readers can learn the order of the incidents in Matthew, and so try the experiment of using what they have learnt to help them meditate their way through the Gospel. This stems from Andrew's conviction that Matthew wrote not only to give us information about Jesus, but also to help us to meet him.

Would you like to give it a try? If your answer is Yes, The Matthew Experiment is the book for you.

ISBN 978-3-95776-069-2
Pb. • 184 pp. • £ 10.00

VTR Publications
info@vtr-online.com
http://www.vtr-online.com

The Mark Experiment

How Mark's Gospel can help you know Jesus better

Andrew Page

If you are looking for a new way into Mark's Gospel and you long to allow the Gospel to help you worship and experience Jesus, *The Mark Experiment* is the book for you.

In *The Mark Experiment* Andrew Page shows you how to commit the Gospel to memory and explains how learning to meditate on the Gospel events has transformed his relationship with Jesus. Think what this might mean for your understanding of the life and ministry of Jesus.

One exciting result of this book has been the development of an innovative drama in which a team of 15 Christians from a church or student group acts out every incident in the Gospel of Mark as theatre-in-the-round. The Mark Drama is now being performed in many countries around the world.

www.themarkdrama.com

ISBN 978-3-937965-21-5
Pb. • 106 pp. • £ 8.00

VTR Publications
info@vtr-online.com
http://www.vtr-online.com

The John Experiment

How John's Gospel can help you know Jesus better

Andrew Page

Are you looking for a new way into the Gospels? Whether you have been a Christian for many years or are just considering the Christian faith, John's Gospel is a great place to start.

In The John Experiment Andrew Page unpacks John's Gospel and shows you how to commit it to memory. He explains how learning to meditate on the Gospel events is transforming his relationship with Jesus.

Would you like to give it a go? If your answer is Yes, then The John Experiment is the book for you.

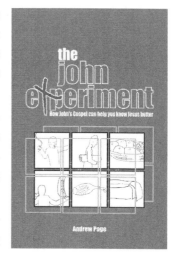

ISBN 978-3-95776-070-8
Pb. • 146 pp. • £ 9.50

VTR Publications
info@vtr-online.com
http://www.vtr-online.com

The 5 Habits of
Deeply Contented People

Andrew Page

Have you found contentment?
Most people are looking for it.
If you're not, it may be because you've given up...

If you are searching or want to start your search again, *The 5 Habits of Deeply Contented People* is the book for you.

The Bible says that everyone is made in God's image. Andrew Page says there are 5 habits which express that image of God in us. He says "If we can work out what these habits mean in practice for us as individuals, we will experience a deeper level of contentment."

Basing what he writes on the second chapter of the Bible, and making clear that these habits work even if we don't believe in God, Andrew invites his readers to try out the habits for themselves.

• Do you want to be more contented, whatever life throws at you?
• Are you curious to know what it means to be made in God's image?
• Would you like to find out if the 5 habits work?

If you have said Yes to any of these questions, *The 5 Habits of Deeply Contented People* is a great place to start.

ISBN 978-3-95776-009-8
Pb. • 52 pp. • £ 7.00

VTR Publications
info@vtr-online.com
http://www.vtr-online.com

How to Teach the Bible so that People Meet God

Andrew Page

Andrew Page believes that Bible teaching can be a supernatural event. A graduate of London School of Theology, Andrew was a missionary in Austria for 20 years, working with the Austrian Christian student movement (IFES) and later pastoring a church in Innsbruck.

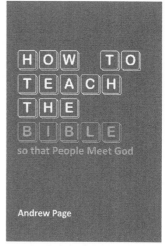

He says "Two enemies of Christian churches are Bible teaching with little biblical content and Bible teaching which is more a lecture than an event." If you agree with this, *How to Teach the Bible so that People Meet God* is the book for you.

This is unashamedly a how-to book. Andrew has trained others in this method of teaching a Bible passage in a number of countries around Europe, and now for the first time the method is available as a book.

So, 3 questions before you buy this book:
• Do you want to find out if God has given you the gift of teaching?
• Do you want to grow in the gift you believe you have?
• Do you want to help a friend to develop as a Bible teacher?

If you have said *Yes* to any of these questions, *How to Teach the Bible so that People Meet God* is a great place to start.

ISBN 978-3-95776-035-7
Pb. • 64 pp. • £ 7.50

VTR Publications
info@vtr-online.com
http://www.vtr-online.com

How to Lead How to Lead Group Bible Study so that People Meet God

Andrew Page

Are you part of a Christian small group? Does your church or CU offer training to those who lead group Bible study? Do you know people who want help in how to prepare and lead group Bible study?

If you are looking for practical training in this area, *How to Lead Group Bible Study so that People Meet God* is the book for you.

Andrew Page believes that small group Bible study can be a supernatural event. A graduate of London School of Theology, Andrew was a missionary in Austria for 20 years, working with the Austrian Christian student movement (IFES) and later pastoring a church in Innsbruck.

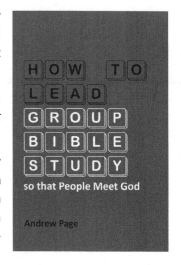

This is unashamedly a how-to book. Andrew has trained many people in Christian Unions and in churches, both in Austria and in the UK, and now for the first time the material is available as a book.

So, 3 questions before you buy this book:
• Do you want to start leading group Bible study?
• If you already lead group Bible study, do you want to do it better?
• Do you want to help others to learn to lead group Bible study?

If you have said Yes to any of these questions, *How to Lead Group Bible Study so that People Meet God* is a great place to start.

ISBN 978-3-95776-130-9
Pb. • 60 pp. • £ 7.50

VTR Publications
info@vtr-online.com
http://www.vtr-online.com